This new 4th edition of *Pyramid* contains the same features you have come to love but is significantly revised and expanded. We have added sixteen pages of new pyramid exercises, forty-two new multisyllable words, an all-new cover, more proverbs, and a beautiful new colored cover.

Pyramid

Written and Illustrated by
Dolores G. Hiskes, President

With everlasting gratitude
to Jean Bacigalupi,
who brightened the lives of so
with her soaring generosity and kind heart.
She was dearly beloved by all the
students and tutors at YES Reading,
and will be greatly missed.

Publisher's Cataloging in Publication
(Prepared by Quality Books, Inc.)
Hiskes, Dolores G.
    Pyramid: special reading exercises / written and
illustrated by Dolores G. Hiskes—4th ed.
    p.cm.
    ISBN:1-884580-32-7
    1. Reading.   I. Title
LB1573.H57   372.4'1   QB196-40435

Dorbooks, Inc.~P.O. Box 2588~Livermore CA 94551
Phone 925-449-6983~Fax 447-6983 (area code may change)
http://www.dorbooks.com~dor@dorbooks.com

Acknowledgements

I am now and will be forever thankful:
for our beloved children Robin and Grant, who inspired
a passion for teaching reading in the very beginning...
for our sweet and innocent grandchildren
who unwittingly serve as guinea pigs for
all of my new material...
and for my beloved and long-suffering husband Johnny,
who knew better than to believe me when
I promised I wouldn't write anymore books
(once again putting up with long and lonely hours
as I hunched over my computer day and night).
Grateful thanks also:
to my talented and gifted illustrator Linda Rogers
for executing my cover design so brilliantly and adding
an idea or two of her own...
to my awesome and eagle-eyed editor Sherrill Fink
for catching all of the obvious errors that I should have caught
and all the subtle ones I wouldn't have,, as well as apologies
for any errors that still lurk, which are all mine
(changes were made after proofing)...
to Rayve Fulfillment and The Intrepid Group for their
wonderful fullfillment service and warm friendship...
to the talented, dedicated tutors at YES Reading in Menlo Park
who have given so generously of their time, talents, and resources
to this extraordinary and inspirational program...
to May May Gong of Northwest Digital Designs
for my stunning web site (www.nwdigitaldesigns.com)...
to Mark McCreary for developing such a great and easy-to-use
e-newsletter computer site (www.mail-list.com)...
and last but certainly not least,
to Jon Kalb, Mark McCreary, May May Gong, George Pavel,
and Chris Ebbers for their amazing
computer savvy
and kind helpfulness.

THANKS!

Go, little book, and wish to all

Flowers in the garden,

Meat in the hall.

A bin of wine, a spice of wit,

A house with lawns enclosing it,

A living river by the door,

A nightingale in the sycamore!

—Robert Louis Stevenson

Introduction

Pyramid was written to provide supplementary practice for *Phonics Pathways* but can be used successfully to enhance any other reading method. This all-new, greatly expanded fourth edition has sixteen added pages: ten pages of new pyramid exercises featuring r-modified vowels and vowel digraphs, and six pages with forty-two added multisyllable words. It also features greatly enhanced graphics, additional proverbs, and a beautiful new colored cover.

Many students need extra help in learning how to track left-to-right with their eyes. Their eye muscles are not sufficiently developed to allow their eyes to move smoothly together from left to right across a page, and so they experience difficulty in reading words and/or sentences. (For more information check out *Phonics Talk*, our informative e-mail newsletter, at http://www.dorbooks.com/phonicstalk.html.)

These students need extra reading practice that gradually and systematically builds letters into words, and words into connected reading. This kind of reading practice develops and strengthens the eye-tracking skill that will allow them to read with ease and fluency, but it can be difficult to find. *Pyramid* provides this kind of practice with graduated "eyerobic" reading exercises—visual aerobics.

Every lesson in the first section of *Pyramid* begins by blending letters into words. Students should know all the letter sounds before beginning *Pyramid*, including all of the short-vowel sounds. If students do know letter sounds but have difficulty reading words, they should limit their initial practice to the top part of the pyramids from pages seven to eleven.

The same words are then built into sentences, beginning with one word centered on top of the page. Every subsequent line has added words, giving it the shape of a pyramid. Each lesson in this section develops a different skill and follows the same basic format as *Phonics Pathways*.

An optional and very useful activity is to write the sentences from dictation—it helps develop auditory and sequencing memory.

Reading should continue as long as students are challenged, but stop at or before frustration level. With practice, they will be able to read longer and longer sentences. Students who continue having prolonged difficulty could have a vision problem that might benefit from the services of a specialist for diagnosis and remediation.

The last section is for established readers who need assistance reading multisyllable words. Longer words are built from smaller ones by syllables into mini-pyramids, and then incorporated into sentences. There are two pyramid words in each sentence. All one hundred and fourteen multisyllable words are summarized on the last page for ongoing reference and use, with the original word highlighted inside of the longer one. Students can effortlessly move into reading multisyllable words when they are graphically illustrated in this way—and they will expand their vocabularies as well. And now—please enjoy *Pyramid!*

~Dolores

Contents

Hi! I'm Dewey the Bookworm,* and I'll be your guide through Pyramid.
When you read a Pyramid exercise, don't feel you have to read the whole thing.
Just go as far as you can, and then come back to it the next day.
Each day you'll be able to read farther and farther down the page—you'll see!

*Dewey D. System, Bookwurmus Giganticus
©1982 Dolores G. Hiskes

Short-Vowel Review

WORDS IN TOP SECTION:

A "diacritical mark" is a symbol on top of a letter that shows us how to pronounce it. There are diacritical marks for many different sounds, but in this book we will only practice the marks for short and long vowel sounds. The diacritical mark for a short-vowel sound is " ˘ ," as in "săt." This particular diacritical mark is called a "breve." There are five pages in this section, with one vowel featured on each page.

Read the words on top of the next page, working from left to right. Make sure that you blend the sounds together smoothly, and do not sound out each separate letter when you read the final word. Then write these words from dictation. This section of *Pyramid* is especially helpful for those of you who know letter sounds but need extra practice blending letters into words. Your left-to-right eye tracking will become *stronger!*

SENTENCES IN BOTTOM SECTION:

After you are able to read these words smoothly and write them without error, you may begin reading the *Pyramid* sentences on the lower half of the page. This section is especially helpful to those of you who already are reading words but need extra practice building words into whole sentences.

Begin with the top word, and read down as many lines as you can. Stop when it becomes too much of an effort. Keep reading this story—you will find that with practice, you will be able to read farther and farther down the page. Your eye span is *increasing!*

Just for fun, youl might try writing these sentences from dictation, as well as the words. It will not only help develop your memory, but also your ability to remember things in the correct order!

Take it easy. Just take one small thing at a time, and keep on going. It's like climbing a large oak tree: you only climb up one branch at a time, but if you keep on going you'll end up on top!

Some people sit on an acorn, waiting for it to grow and carry them to the top. Guess what......they are still waiting!

/ks/

Ă ă

c-a	ca	ca-t	cat	
f-a	fa	fa-t	fat	
s-a	sa	sa-t	sat	
h-a	ha	ha-t	hat	/Maks/
M-a	Ma	Ma-x	Max	Max-'s
J-a	Ja	Ja-n	Jan	Jan-'s

Jan's

Jan's cat

Jan's fat cat

Jan's fat cat sat.

Jan's fat cat sat on Max.

Jan's fat cat sat on Max's hat!

Only the COMPLETE SENTENCES have periods at the end— the rest of the lines are only PHRASES.

Ĕ ĕ

b-e	be	be-d	bed	
g-e	ge	ge-t	get	
f-e	fe	fe-d	fed	
t-e	te	te-n	ten	
p-e	pe	pe-t	pet	pet-s
M-e	Me	Me-l	Mel	Mel-'s

The BEST ANGLE to approach ANY problem is the TRY-ANGLE!

Mel

Mel's pets

Mel's ten pets

Mel's ten pets get

Mel's ten pets get fed.

Mel's ten pets get fed in bed!

Ĭ ĭ

i-n	in			
K-i	Ki	Ki-t	Kit	
h-i	hi	hi-d	hid	
w-i	wi	wi-g	wig	
d-i	di	di-sh	dish	
J-i	Ji	Ji-m	Jim-'s	Jim's
R-i	Ri	Ri-ck	Rick-'s	Rick's

If you ever need help reading a word from the original list, as shown above. this book, as needed. EVERYONE helps a LOT to have them broken

in these sentences, try reading it again Do this for the rest of the sentences in finds SOME words difficult, and it down by syllables or letters!

Kit

Kit hid.

Kit hid Jim's

Kit hid Jim's wig.

Kit hid Jim's wig in Rick's

Kit hid Jim's wig in Rick's dish!

Ŏ ŏ

o-n	on			
B-o	Bo	Bo-b	Bob	
h-o	ho	ho-t	hot	
h-o	ho	ho-p	hop	hop-s
r-o	ro	ro-ck	rock	rock-s
s-o	so	so-ck	sock	sock-s

*The noblest of all dogs is the HOT DOG...
It FEEDS the hand that BITES it!*

Bob

Bob hops.

Bob hops on

Bob hops on hot

Bob hops on hot rocks.

Bob hops on hot rocks in socks!

u-g	ug	ug-ly	ugly	
p-u	pu	pu-p	pup	
d-u	du	du-g	dug	
s-u	su	su-ch	such	
b-u	bu	bu-g	bug	bug-s
B-u	Bu	Bu-d	Bud	Bud-'s

Ŭ ŭ

*The door to the human heart can only be opened from the **INSIDE!!!***

Bud

Bud's pup

Bud's pup dug.

Bud's pup dug such

Bud's pup dug such ugly

Bud's pup dug such ugly bugs!

Short-Vowel Pyramids

The following *Pyramid*s contain all of the short-vowel sounds mixed together, and the sentences are longer as well. First read the words on this page, working from left to right. Each "block" of words on this page has the same short-vowel sound. Then write these words from dictation.

After you are able to read these words smoothly and spell them correctly, you may begin reading the *Pyramid* on the next page. There is one sight word in *Pyramid*: it is the word "a."

(Try writing a sentence or two from dictation, also. See how far you can get!)

a	a-n	an	an-d	and	
e	M-e	Me	Me-g	Meg	
i	i-n	in			
i	s-i	si	si-t	sit	sit-s
i	s-i	si	si-p	sip	sip-s
o	h-o	ho	ho-t	hot	
o	p-o	po	po-p	pop	
u	m-u	mu	mu-g	mug	
u	s-u	su	su-n	sun	

NEVER compare yourself with anyone else...
After all, if only the best birds sang,
The woods would be SILENT!

sip

Sip pop.

Meg sips pop.

Meg sits and sips pop.

Meg sits in sun and sips pop.

Meg sits in sun and sips pop in a mug.

Meg sits in hot sun and sips pop in a mug.

Meg sits in hot sun and sips *hot pop* in a mug!

Continue working through the rest of these Pyramids, just as you have on pages 12 and 13. Take your time— there is no hurry. Sometimes it takes the most beautiful flowers in the garden the longest to grow!

a	f-a	fa	fa-t	fat
a	h-a	ha	ha-s	has
a	b-a	ba	ba-ck	back
e	K-e	Ke	Ke-n	Ken
e	d-e	de	de-ck	deck
i	b-i	bi	bi-g	big
i	h-i	hi	hi-s	his
o	o-n	on		
u	d-u	du	du-ck	duck

Blessed are the FLEXIBLE...
For they shall not
be BENT out of SHAPE!

Ken

Ken has

Ken has a deck.

Ken has a back deck.

Ken has a big back deck.

Ken has a duck on his back deck.

Ken has a fat duck on his back deck.

Ken has a big fat duck on his back deck.

Ken has a big fat duck on his big back deck!

a	J-a	Ja	Ja-n	Jan	
a	P-a	Pa	Pa-t	Pat	
a	a-n	an	an-d	and	

e	w-e	we	we-t	wet

i	s-i	si	si-t	sit
i	d-i	di	di-g	dig

o	T-o	To	To-m	Tom	
o	j-o	jo	jo-g	jog	
o	h-o	ho	ho-p	hop	
o	h-o	ho	ho-p	hop	hop-s

u	b-u	bu	bu-g	bug	bug-s

It's a REAL CHALLENGE
to climb the ladder of success...
For you must keep your:
EYES on the ball,
EARS to the ground,
NOSE to the grindstone,
HANDS on the wheel, and
FEET on the path...
But the view from the top is
FANTASTIC!!!

PEAK OF SUCCESS

hop

Jan hops.

Jan and Tom hop.

Jan, Pat, and Tom hop.

Jan, Pat, and Tom hop and jog.

Jan, Pat, and Tom hop, jog, and sit.

Jan, Pat, and Tom hop, jog, sit, and dig.

Jan, Pat, and Tom hop, jog, sit, and dig *wet bugs!*

17

> *There's so much good*
> *in the WORST of us,*
> *And so much bad*
> *in the BEST of us,*
> *That it hardly behooves*
> *ANY of us*
> *To talk about*
> *the REST of us!*

a	h-a	ha	ha-m	ham	
a	j-a	ja	ja-m	jam	
a	a-n	an	an-d	and	
a	a-n	an	an-t	ant	ant-s

e	f-e	fe	fe-d	fed
e	B-e	Be	Be-n	Ben
e	r-e	re	re-d	red

| i | b-i | bi | bi-g | big |

| o | h-o | ho | ho-t | hot |

| u | G-u | Gu | Gu-s | Gus | |
| u | b-u | bu | bu-n | bun | bun-s |

Some people are so afraid of ROCKING THE BOAT
That they STOP ROWING!

fed

fed Gus

Ben fed Gus.

Ben fed Gus jam.

Ben fed Gus red jam.

Ben fed Gus red jam and buns.

Ben fed Gus red jam and hot buns.

Ben fed Gus red jam, hot buns, and ham.

Ben fed Gus red jam, hot buns, ham, and *big ants!*

> *The road UPHILL*
> *And the road DOWNHILL*
> *are the same one!*

a	h-a	ha	ha-d	had	
a	b-a	ba	ba-g	bag	
a	a-n	an	an-d	and	
a	c-a	ca	ca-t	cat	
a	f-a	fa	fa-t	fat	

i	i-n	in			
i	h-i	hi	hi-d	hid	
i	h-i	hi	hi-s	his	
i	b-i	bi	bi-g	big	
i	f-i	fi	fi-g	fig	fig-s

o	B-o	Bo	Bo-b	Bob	

u	g-u	gu	gu-m	gum	
u	n-u	nu	nu-t	nut	nut-s

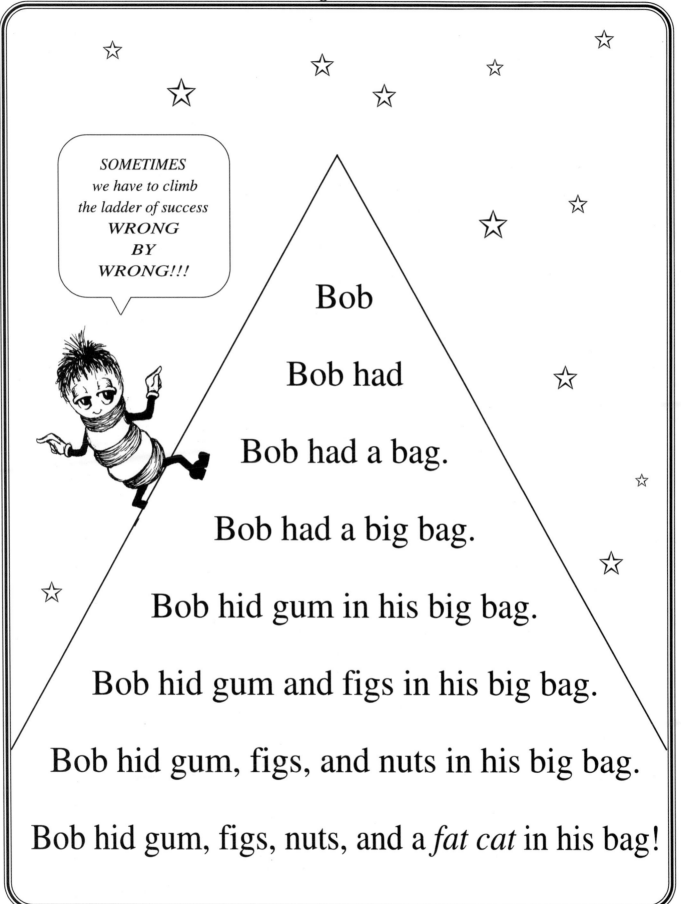

SOMETIMES
we have to climb
the ladder of success
WRONG
BY
WRONG!!!

Bob

Bob had

Bob had a bag.

Bob had a big bag.

Bob hid gum in his big bag.

Bob hid gum and figs in his big bag.

Bob hid gum, figs, and nuts in his big bag.

Bob hid gum, figs, nuts, and a *fat cat* in his bag!

a	c-a	ca	ca-t	cat
a	a-n	an	an-d	and
a	s-a	sa	sa-d	sad
a	f-a	fa	fa-t	fat
a	S-a	Sa	Sa-m	Sam

| e | r-e | re | re-d | red |

i	i-s	is		
i	k-i	ki	ki-ss	kiss
i	J-i	Ji	Ji-ll	Jill

| o | n-o | ho | no-t | not |
| o | l-o | lo | lo-t | lot |

u	G-u	Gu	Gu-s	Gus
u	h-u	hu	hu-g	hug
u	P-u	Pu	Pu-ff	Puff

Bad habits are like a comfortable BED...
Easy to get INTO, but hard to get OUT of!

Puff

Puff is

Puff is a cat.

Puff is a fat cat.

Puff is a fat, red cat.

Jill and Sam kiss fat Puff.

Jill and Sam hug and kiss fat Puff.

Jill and Sam hug Puff a lot, and Gus is sad.

Jill and Sam hug and kiss Gus, and Gus is *not* sad!

ACT *the way you want to* BE,
And soon you'll BE *the way you* ACT!

a	a-n	an	an-d	and
a	c-a	ca	ca-t	cat
a	f-a	fa	fa-t	fat
a	l-a	la	la-p	lap
a	m-a	ma	ma-d	mad

| e | w-e | we | we-t | wet |

i	i-n	in		
i	i-s	is		
i	b-i	bi	bi-g	big
i	J-i	Ji	Ji-ll	Jill	Jill-'s

| o | h-o | ho | ho-t | hot | |
| o | h-o | ho | ho-p | hop | hop-s |

| u | P-u | Pu | Pu-ff | Puff |
| u | t-u | tu | tu-b | tub |

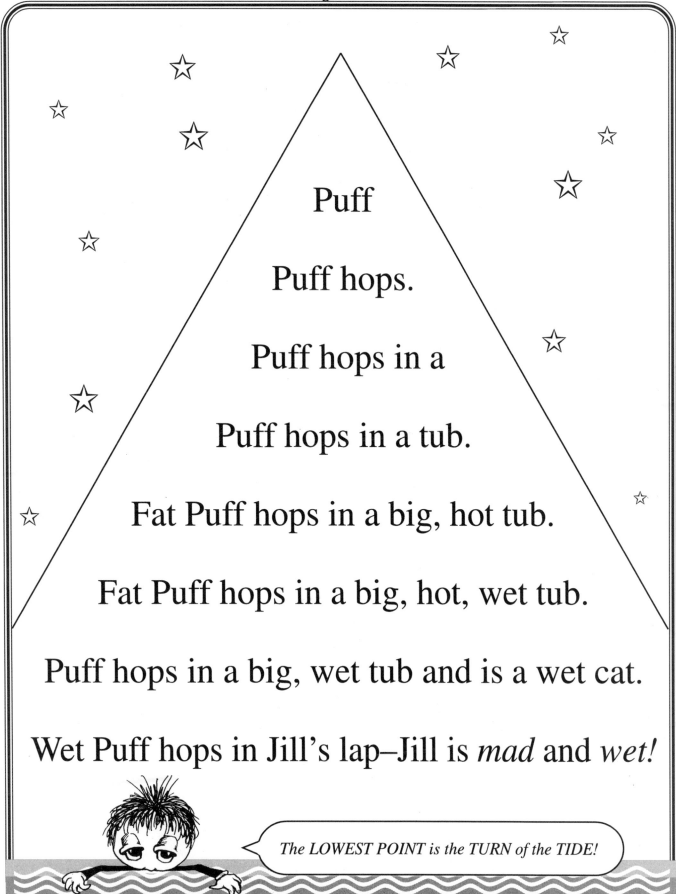

Puff

Puff hops.

Puff hops in a

Puff hops in a tub.

Fat Puff hops in a big, hot tub.

Fat Puff hops in a big, hot, wet tub.

Puff hops in a big, wet tub and is a wet cat.

Wet Puff hops in Jill's lap–Jill is *mad* and *wet!*

The LOWEST POINT is the TURN of the TIDE!

Life is a GRINDSTONE . . .
But whether it grinds us down
Or polishes us up
Depends on US!
(Oh yes, we have another sight word
in the next Pyramid—"he.")

a	a-s	as			
a	f-a	fa	fa-t	fat	
a	a-n	an	an-d	and	
a	t-a	ta	ta-n	tan	
a	n-a	na	na-p	nap	nap-s

| e | g-e | ge | ge-t | get-s | gets |

i	i-s	is		
i	i-n	in		
i	p-i	pi	pi-g	pig

| o | h-o | ho | ho-t | hot |

| u | G-u | Gu | Gu-s | Gus |
| u | s-u | su | su-n | sun |

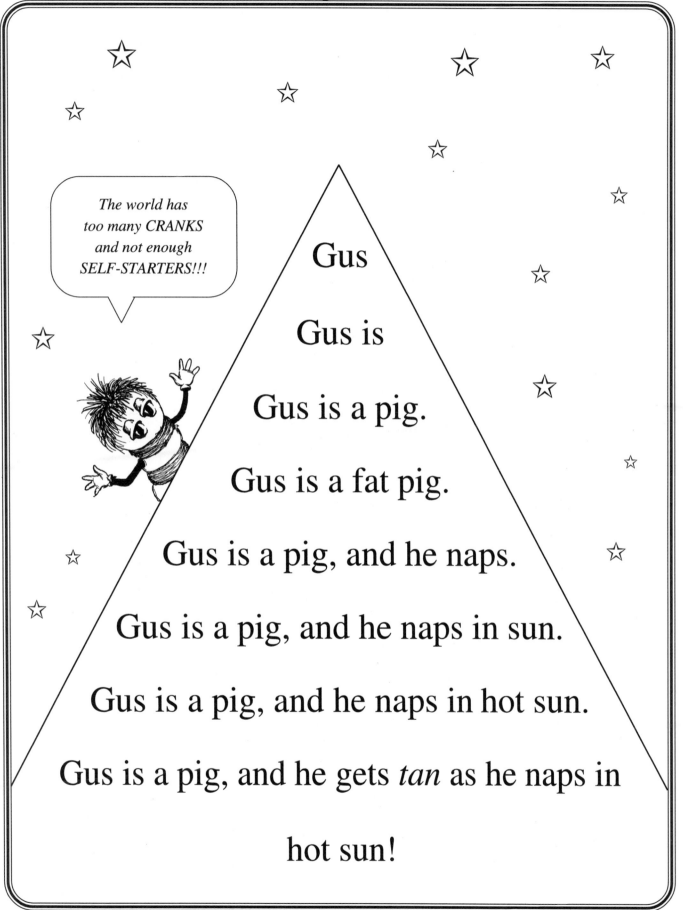

The world has
too many CRANKS
and not enough
SELF-STARTERS!!!

Gus

Gus is

Gus is a pig.

Gus is a fat pig.

Gus is a pig, and he naps.

Gus is a pig, and he naps in sun.

Gus is a pig, and he naps in hot sun.

Gus is a pig, and he gets *tan* as he naps in

hot sun!

Double-Consonant Endings
(Short-Vowel Words)

a	f-a	fa	fa-t	fat	
a	a-n	an	an-d	and	
a	b-a	ba	ba-d	bad	
a	n-a	na	na-p	nap	
a	J-a	Ja	Ja-ck	Jack	Jack's

e	b-e	be	be-d	bed	
e	r-e	re	re-s	res	res-t

i	i-s	is			
i	i-n	in			
i	w-i	wi	wi-th	with	
i	s-i	si	si-ck	sick	

We can't ALL be shining examples, but we can at least TWINKLE a little!!!

o	h-o	ho	ho-p	hops	

u	b-u	bu	bu-g	bug	
u	G-u	Gu	Gu-s	Gus	
u	m-u	mu	mu-s	mus	mus-t
u	b-u	bu	bu-m	bum	bum-p
u	l-u	lu	lu-m	lum	lum-py

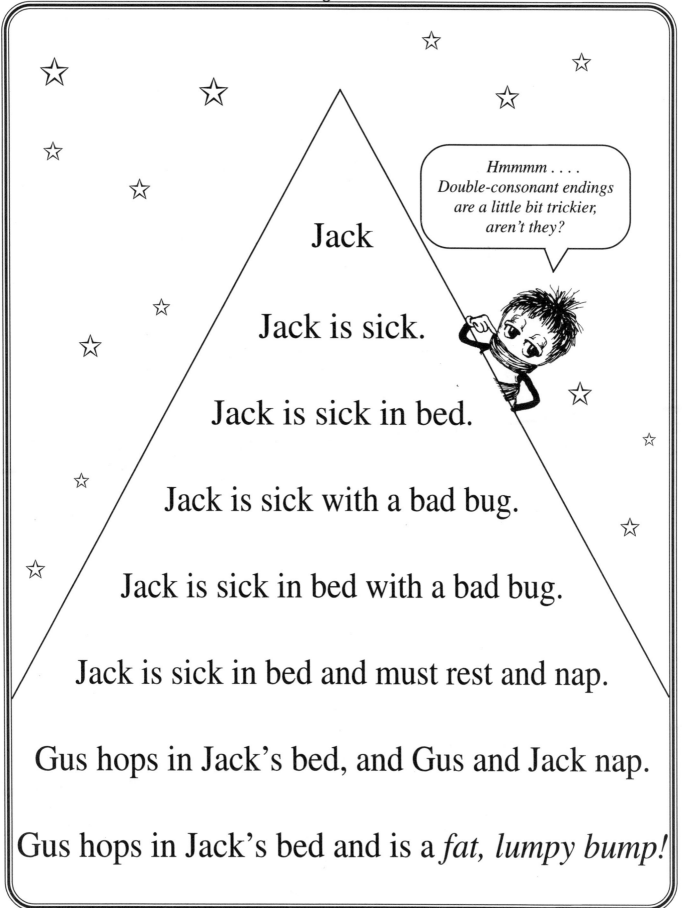

Jack

Jack is sick.

*Hmmmm . . . .
Double-consonant endings
are a little bit trickier,
aren't they?*

Jack is sick in bed.

Jack is sick with a bad bug.

Jack is sick in bed with a bad bug.

Jack is sick in bed and must rest and nap.

Gus hops in Jack's bed, and Gus and Jack nap.

Gus hops in Jack's bed and is a *fat, lumpy bump!*

| a | a-n | an | an-d | and | |
| a | f-a | fa | fa-t | fat | |

| e | f-e | fe | fe-ll | fell | |
| e | S-e | Se | Se-th | Seth | |

i	b-i	bi	bi-g	big	
i	l-i	li	li-p	lip	
i	h-i	hi	hi-ll	hill	

o	o-n	on			
o	h-o	ho	ho-p	hop	hop-s
o	r-o	ro	ro-ck	rock	

u	u-p	up			
u	c-u	cu	cu-t	cut	
u	b-u	bu	bu-m	bum	bum-py

Whether you are climbing to the peak of a mountain or the peak of literacy, you simply take one small step at a time, and keep on going, right to the
TOP!!!

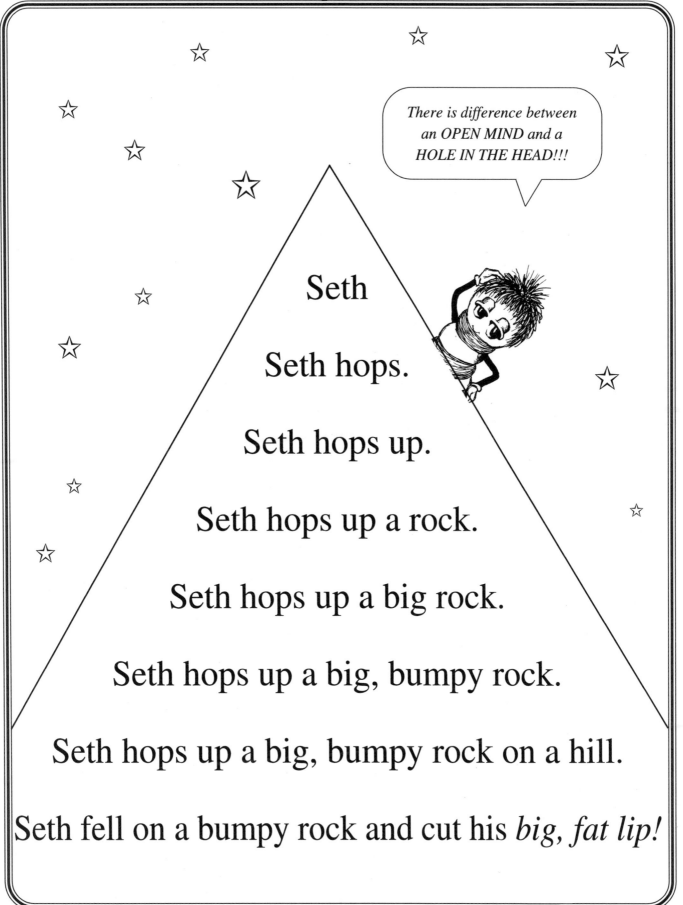

There is difference between an OPEN MIND and a HOLE IN THE HEAD!!!

Seth

Seth hops.

Seth hops up.

Seth hops up a rock.

Seth hops up a big rock.

Seth hops up a big, bumpy rock.

Seth hops up a big, bumpy rock on a hill.

Seth fell on a bumpy rock and cut his *big, fat lip!*

Make your life a light to others...
A candle loses nothing of its light
by lighting another candle...
Brighten the corner where YOU are!

a	a-t	at				
a	a-n	an	an-d	and		
a	p-a	pa	pa-s	pas	pas-t	past
a	p-a	pa	pa-th	path		
a	r-a	ra	ra-n	ran	ran-ch	ranch

| e | B-e | Be | Be-th | Beth | | |
| e | K-e | Ke | Ke-n | Ken | Ken-t | Kent-'s |

i	i-n	in		
i	b-i	bi	bi-g	
i	R-i	Ri	Ri-ck	Rick

| o | p-o | po | po-n | pon | pon-d | pond |

u	d-u	du	du-ck	duck		
u	j-u	ju	ju-s	jus-t	just	
u	j-u	ju	ju-m	jum	jum-p	jump

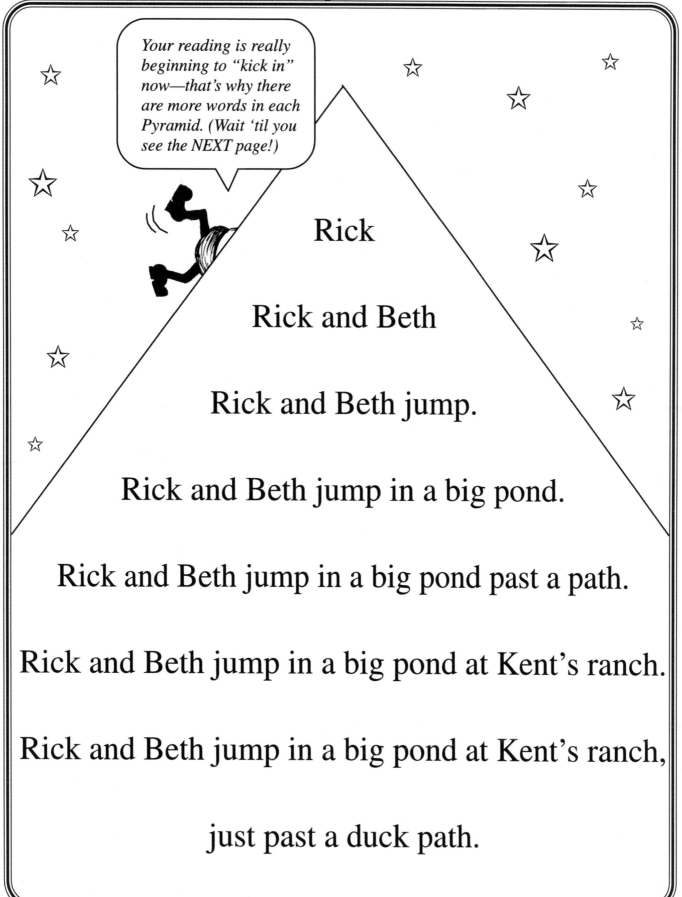

Your reading is really beginning to "kick in" now—that's why there are more words in each Pyramid. (Wait 'til you see the NEXT page!)

Rick

Rick and Beth

Rick and Beth jump.

Rick and Beth jump in a big pond.

Rick and Beth jump in a big pond past a path.

Rick and Beth jump in a big pond at Kent's ranch.

Rick and Beth jump in a big pond at Kent's ranch,

just past a duck path.

a	a-n	an	an-d	and		
a	s-a	sa	sa-n	san	san-d	sand
a	h-a	ha	ha-n	han	han-d	hand
a	c-a	ca	ca-s	cas	cas-k	cask

e	t-e	te	te-n	ten		
e	K-e	Ke	Ke-n	Ken	Ken-t	Kent
e	f-e	fe	fe-l	fel	fel-t	felt
e	y-e	ye	ye-l	yel	yel-ps	yelps

i	i-s	is				
i	i-n	in				
i	b-i	bi	bi-g	big		
i	h-i	hi	hi-s	his		
i	w-i	wi	wi-th	with		
i	m-i	mi	mi-l	mil	mil-k	milk
i	m-i	mi	mi-n	min	min-ts	mints
i	l-i	li	li-f	lif	lif-ts	lifts
i	f-i	fi	fi-ll	fill	fill-ed	filled

See what I MEAN???

u	d-u	du	du-g	dug		
u	l-u	lu	lu-m	lum	lum-p	lump
u	j-u	ju	ju-s	jus	jus-t	just
u	g-u	gu	gu-l	gul	gul-ps	gulps

Kindness costs NOTHING...
But the things that it buys
are PRICELESS!!!

Kent

Kent dug

Kent dug in sand.

Kent dug his hand in sand.

Kent dug in sand and felt a lump.

Kent lifts a big lump with his hands.

His lump is a big cask filled with mints.

Kent's big cask is just *filled* with big mints!

Kent yelps and gulps ten big mints with milk.

Long-Vowel Review

The *Pyramids* in this section are all comprised of long-vowel sounds.
The diacritical mark for a long-vowel sound is " ¯ ," as in "sāme."
A long-vowel diacritical mark is called a "macron."

First read the words on top of the next page, working from left to right.
Remember to blend the sounds together smoothly!

Then write the words from dictation.

After you are able to read these words smoothly and write them without error,
you may begin reading the *Pyramid* sentences on the bottom of the page.

Begin with the top word, as we have been doing, and continue reading down
the page. With practice, you will be able to read farther and farther down the
page—perhaps even the very last sentence! (But don't worry if you can't—
just do the best that you can.)

The long-vowel words in this section of *Pyramid* are all "silent-e" words—
that is, they all have an "e" on the end, which changes the vowel from short
to long.* There are five pages in this section and one vowel to each page.

(Remember—try writing a few sentences from dictation, as well as words.)

*Here are some examples of three-letter words
using each short vowel. Notice how adding the
"silent e" changes them to long vowel words:*

(a) păn + e = pāne
(e) pĕt + e = Pēte
(i) bĭt + e = bīte
(o) hŏp + e = hōpe
(u) cŭt + e = cūte

36

Āā

a-te	ate			
d-a	da	da-te	date	
c-a	ca	ca-ke	cake	
D-a	Da	Da-ve	Dave	
l-a	la	p-la	pla	pla-te
J-a	Ja	Ja-ne	Jane	Jane-'s

TRYING times are not the times to STOP trying!!!

Dave

Dave ate.

Dave ate Jane's

Dave ate Jane's plate

Dave ate Jane's plate of date

Dave ate Jane's plate of date cake.

Ēē

P-e	Pe	Pe-te	Pete	
l-ea	lea	lea-n	lean	
l-ea	lea	lea-p	leap	
m-ea	mea	mea-n	mean	
l-ee	lee	f-lee	flee	flee-s
l-ea	lea	f-lea	flea	flea-s

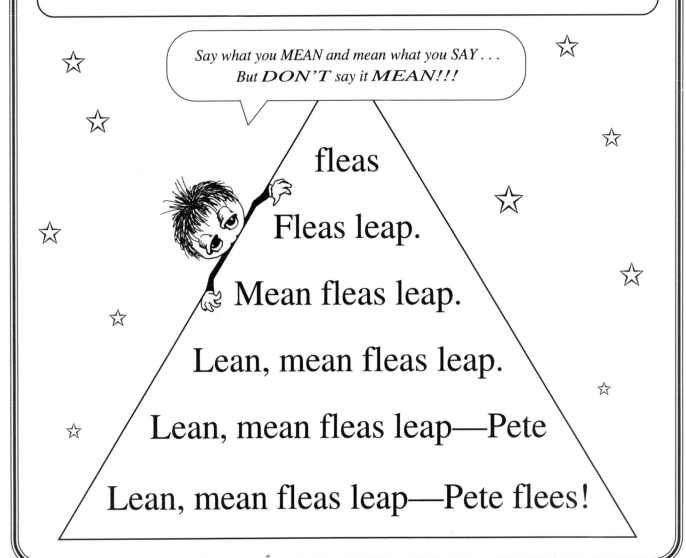

Say what you MEAN and mean what you SAY . . .
*But **DON'T** say it **MEAN**!!!*

fleas

Fleas leap.

Mean fleas leap.

Lean, mean fleas leap.

Lean, mean fleas leap—Pete

Lean, mean fleas leap—Pete flees!

Ī ī

M-i	Mi	Mi-ke	Mike	
f-i	fi	fi-ve	five	
n-i	ni	ni-ce	nice	
p-i	pi	pi-ne	pine	pine-s
h-i	hi	hi-ke	hike	hike-s
m-i	mi	mi-le	mile	mile-s

*The world is a **GREAT BOOK**...but those who never venture beyond their own horizons read only **ONE PAGE**...*

Mike

Mike hikes.

Mike hikes five

Mike hikes five miles.

Mike hikes five miles in nice

Mike hikes five miles in nice pines.

Ōō

o-l	ol	ol-d	old	
R-o	Ro	Ro-se	Rose	
w-o	wo	wo-ke	woke	
t-o	to	to-l	tol	tol-d
j-o	jo	jo-ke	joke	joke-s
d-o	do	do-ze	doze	doze-d

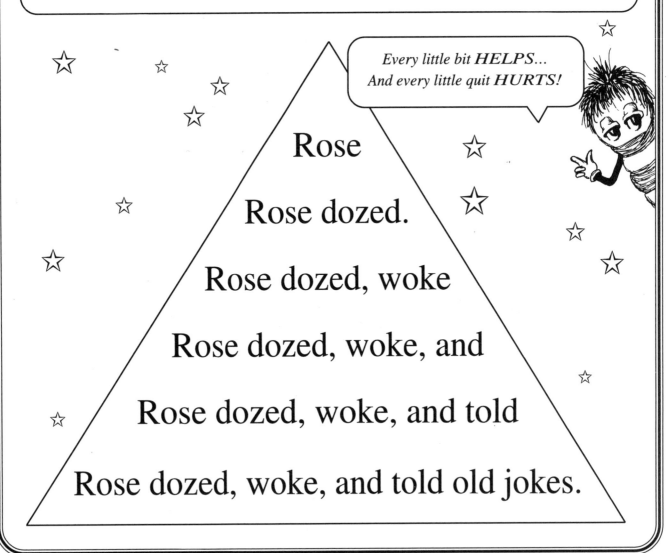

Every little bit HELPS...
And every little quit HURTS!

Rose

Rose dozed.

Rose dozed, woke

Rose dozed, woke, and

Rose dozed, woke, and told

Rose dozed, woke, and told old jokes.

Ūū

u-se	use		
c-u	cu	cu-te	cute
L-u	Lu	Lu-ke	Luke
J-u	Ju	Ju-ne	June
D-u	Du	Du-ke	Duke
m-u	mu	mu-le	mule	mule-s

Be bold in what you STAND FOR . . .
But be careful in what you FALL for!!!

Luke

Luke, June

Luke, June and

Luke, June, and Duke

Luke, June, and Duke use cute

Luke, June, and Duke use cute mules.

Long-Vowel Pyramids

Read the words on this page first, as before. When you are able to read them easily and spell them correctly, you may begin reading the *Pyramid* on the next page. From now on, some of these *Pyramids* will have both long and short-vowel words. Whenever this is the case, diacritical marks will be shown to help you read them.

Hmmm . . . . . .
That looks pretty hard.
Too much WORK to try . . .

(Which Dewey are *you?*)

Hmmm . . . . . .
That looks pretty hard.
Might be FUN to try!

ă	a-t	at			
ā	c-a	ca	ca-ve	cave	
ā	l-a	la	la-ke	lake	
ā	c-a	ca	ca-se	case	

| ēe | d-ee | dee | dee-p | deep | |
| ēe | k-ee | kee | kee-p | keep | keep-s |

ĭ	i-n	in			
ī	p-i	pi	pi-ne	pine	
ī	p-i	pi	pi-le	pile	
ī	d-i	di	di-me	dime	dime-s

| ō | c-o | co | co-ne | cone | cone-s |

| ū | J-u | Ju | Ju-ne | June | |

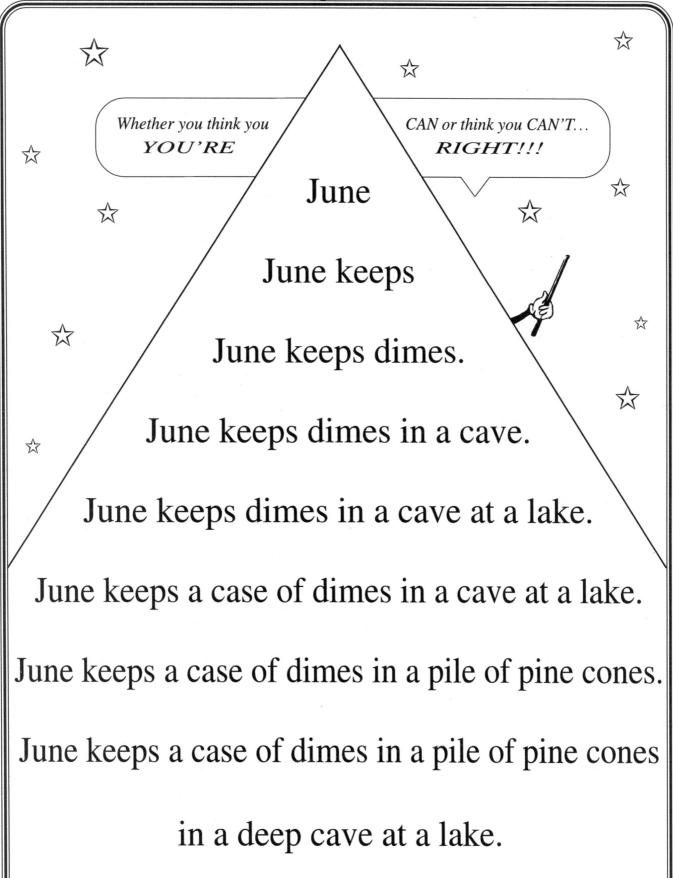

Whether you think you
YOU'RE
CAN or think you CAN'T…
RIGHT!!!

June

June keeps

June keeps dimes.

June keeps dimes in a cave.

June keeps dimes in a cave at a lake.

June keeps a case of dimes in a cave at a lake.

June keeps a case of dimes in a pile of pine cones.

June keeps a case of dimes in a pile of pine cones

in a deep cave at a lake.

a	K-a	Ka	Ka-te	Kate	
a	m-a	ma	ma-ke	make	
a	c-a	ca	ca-ke	cake	
a	t-a	ta	ta-ke	take	take-s

ea	t-ea	tea			
ee	s-ee	see	see-s	sees	
ea	ea-t	eat	eat-s	eats	
ea	m-ea	mea	mea-l	meal	
ea	b-ea	bea	bea-n	bean	bean-s

i	f-i	fi	fi-ne	fine	
i	b-i	bi	bi-te	bite	bite-s
i	l-i	li	li-me	lime	lime-s
i	wh-i	whi	whi-te	white	

o	h-o	ho	ho-me	home
o	J-o	Jo	Jo-dy	Jody

u	L-u	Lu	Lu-ke	Luke

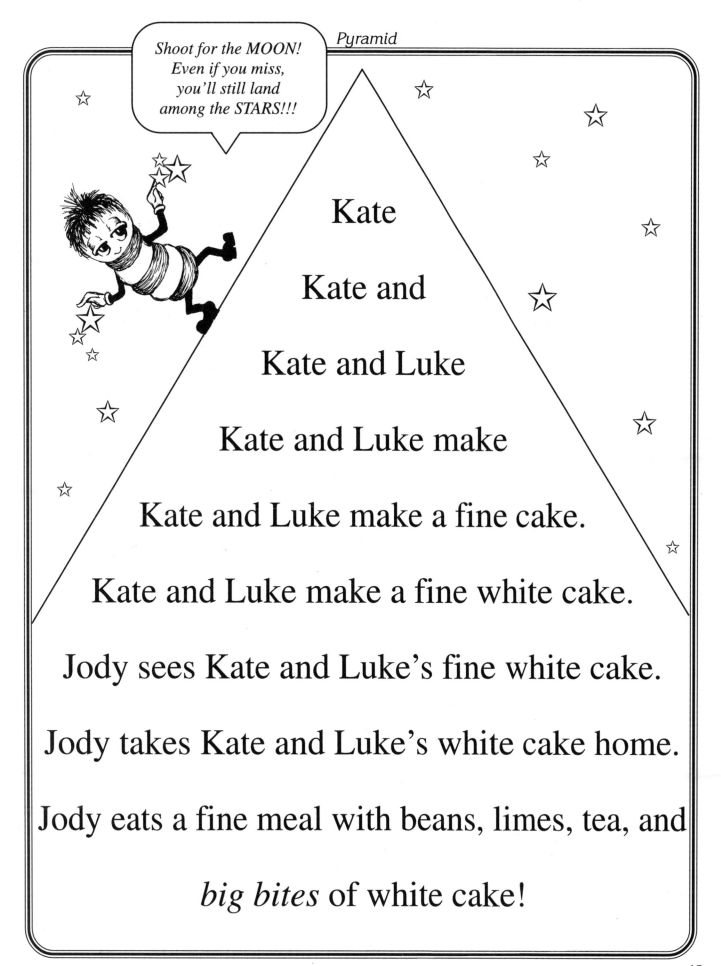

Shoot for the MOON!
Even if you miss,
you'll still land
among the STARS!!!

Kate

Kate and

Kate and Luke

Kate and Luke make

Kate and Luke make a fine cake.

Kate and Luke make a fine white cake.

Jody sees Kate and Luke's fine white cake.

Jody takes Kate and Luke's white cake home.

Jody eats a fine meal with beans, limes, tea, and

big bites of white cake!

Oh no! The sentence on the bottom of the NEXT page is THREE LINES LONG! It could take FOREVER!

But I do wonder what it says? Maybe it can't hurt to try . . . Hmmmmmmmm . . .

What do YOU think??

a	D-a	Da	Da-ve	Dave
a	b-a	ba	ba-ke	bake
a	d-a	da	da-te	date
a	pl-a	pla	pla-te	plate-s
e	sh-ee	shee	shee-t	sheet-s
e	p-ea	pea	pea-ch	peach
e	t-ea	tea	tea-ch	teach
i	f-i	fi	fi-ve	five
i	n-i	ni	ni-ne	nine
i	t-i	ti	ti-ny	tiny
i	M-i	Mi	Mike	
u	R-u	Ru	Ru-th	Ruth
oo	c-oo	coo	coo-k	cook-ies

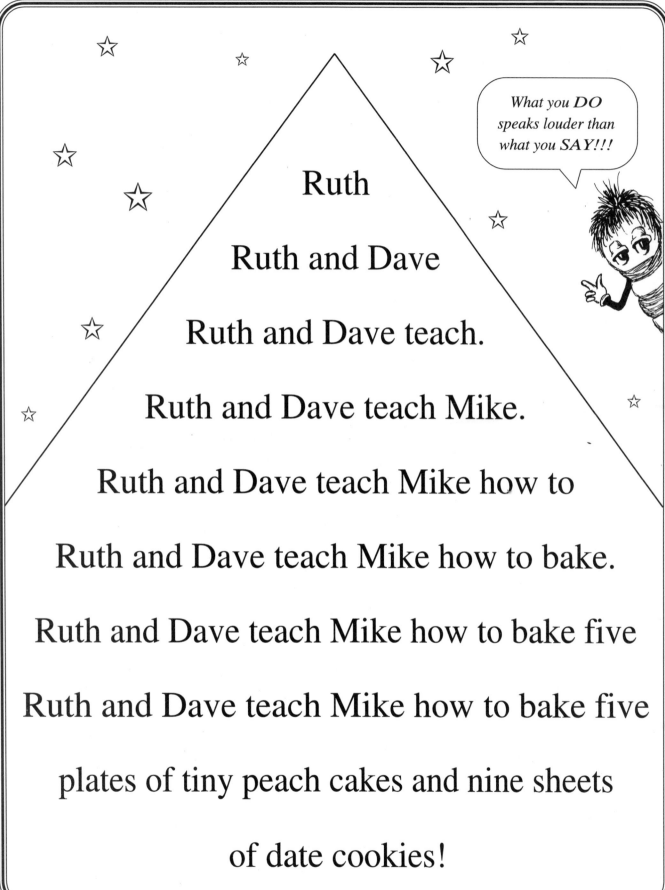

Ruth

Ruth and Dave

Ruth and Dave teach.

Ruth and Dave teach Mike.

Ruth and Dave teach Mike how to

Ruth and Dave teach Mike how to bake.

Ruth and Dave teach Mike how to bake five

Ruth and Dave teach Mike how to bake five

plates of tiny peach cakes and nine sheets

of date cookies!

What you DO speaks louder than what you SAY!!!

Troubles are like BABIES . . .
They only grow if you NURSE them!!!

a	t-a	ta	tak-ing	taking
a	b-a	ba	ba-by	baby
a	sh-a	sha	sha-dy	shady
a	l-a	la	la-ke	lake

| ea | J-ea | Jea | Jea-n | Jean |
| ea | b-ea | bea | bea-ch | beach |

i	l-i	li	li-kes	likes
i	M-i	Mi	Mi-ke	Mike
i	n-i	ni	ni-ce	nice

| o | m-o | mo | mo-st | most-ly |

| u | J-u | Ju | Ju-ne | June |

*If you think you're TOO LITTLE
to make a difference,
Try getting in bed with a MOSQUITO!!*

Jean

Jean likes

Jean mostly likes

Jean mostly likes taking

Jean mostly likes taking baby

Jean mostly likes taking baby Mike to

Jean mostly likes taking baby Mike to the

Jean mostly likes taking baby Mike to the nice

Jean mostly likes taking baby Mike to the nice,

shady beach at June Lake.

Double-Consonant Beginnings
(Short and Long-Vowel Words)

F-r	Fr	Fr-ă	Fra	Fra-n	Fran-'s
b-l	bl	bl-ă	bla	bla-ck	black
t-r	tr	tr-ă	tra	tra-ck	track
b-r	br	br-ā	bra	bra-ke	brake-s
t-r	tr	tr-āi	trai	trai-n	train
s-c	sc	sc-r	scr-ēe	scree-ch	screech-es
s-k	sk	sk-ĭ	ski	ski-d	skid-s
b-r	br	br-ĭ	bri	bri-m	brim
s-l	sl	sl-ĭ	sli	sli-ck	slick
s-k	sk	sk-ĭ	ski	ski-d	skid-s
s-t	st	st-ŏ	sto	sto-p	stop
b-r	br	br-ō	bro	bro-ke	bro-ken

ai - /ā/

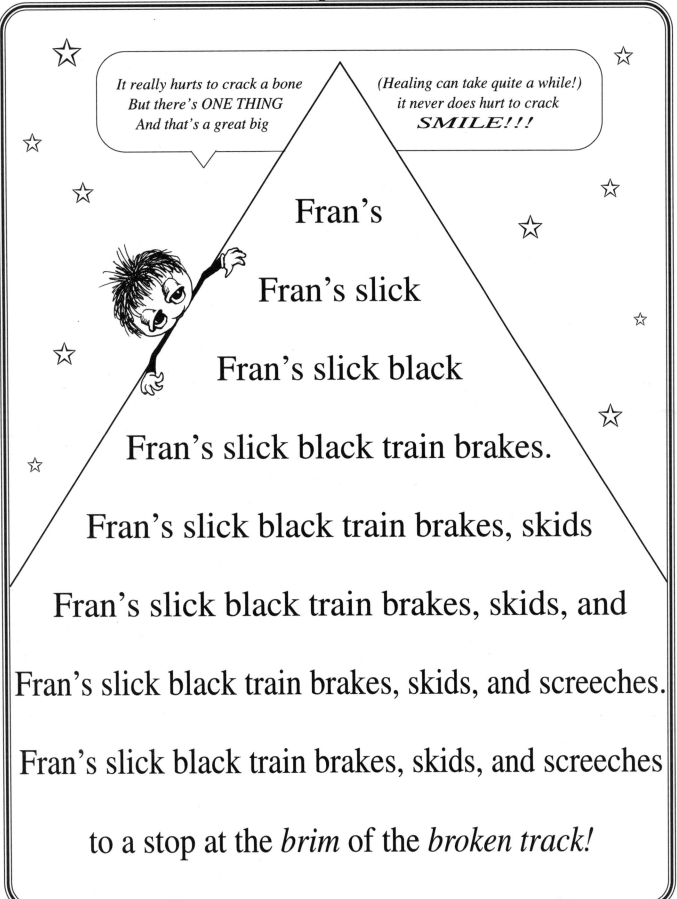

It really hurts to crack a bone
But there's ONE THING
And that's a great big

(Healing can take quite a while!)
it never does hurt to crack
SMILE!!!

Fran's

Fran's slick

Fran's slick black

Fran's slick black train brakes.

Fran's slick black train brakes, skids

Fran's slick black train brakes, skids, and

Fran's slick black train brakes, skids, and screeches.

Fran's slick black train brakes, skids, and screeches

to a stop at the *brim* of the *broken track!*

> Some people see DIFFICULTY
> in every opportunity...
> Others see OPPORTUNITY
> in every difficulty!!!

G-r	Gr	Gr-ă	Gra	Gra-nt	Grant
c-r	cr	cr-ă	cra	cra-ck	crack
c-r	cr	cr-ă	cra	cra-g	crag-gy
c-r	cr	cr-ĕ	cre	cre-st	crest
s-t	st	st-ēe	stee	stee-p	steep
c-l	cl	cl-ĭ	cli	cli-ff	cliff
c-l	cl	cl-ĭ	cli	cli-ng	cling-s
g-r	gr	gr-ō	gro	gro-pe	grope-s
b-r	br	br-ŭ	bru	bru-sh	brush-y

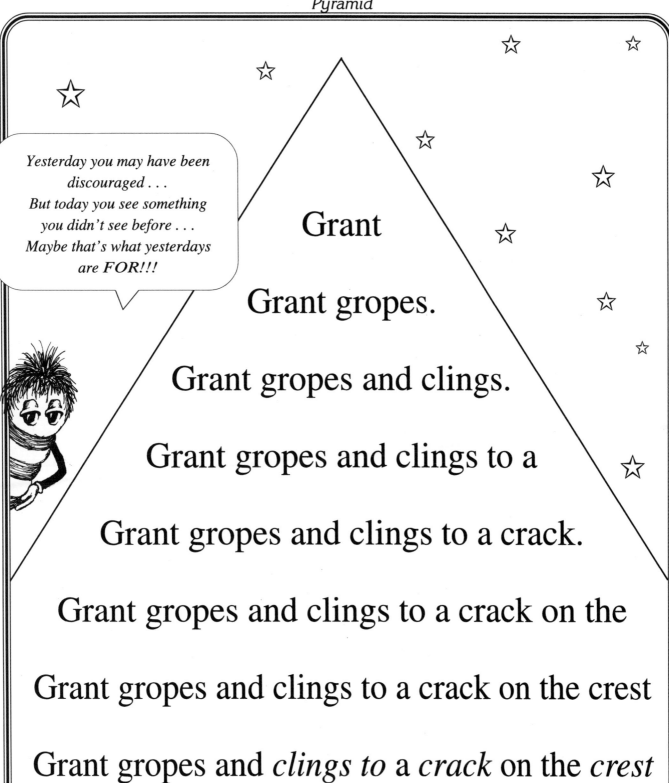

Yesterday you may have been
discouraged . . .
But today you see something
you didn't see before . . .
Maybe that's what yesterdays
are FOR!!!

Grant

Grant gropes.

Grant gropes and clings.

Grant gropes and clings to a

Grant gropes and clings to a crack.

Grant gropes and clings to a crack on the

Grant gropes and clings to a crack on the crest

Grant gropes and *clings to* a *crack* on the *crest*

of the craggy, brushy, *steep cliff!*

On the bottom of the next page you will find the
LONGEST SENTENCE
in this entire book! (I wonder how far you'll get?)

s-t	st	st-ĕ	ste	ste-p	step
c-r	cr	cr-ēe	cree	cree-p	creep
s-l	sl	sl-ēe	slee	slee-p	sleep

s-l	sl	sl-ĭ	sli	sli-p	slip
t-r	tr	tr-ĭ	tri	tri-p	trip
f-l	fl	fl-ĭ	fli	fli-p	flip
s-k	sk	sk-ĭ	ski	ski-d	skid
s-p	sp	sp-ĭ	spi	spi-n	spin
s-l	sl	sl-ī	sli	sli-de	slide
f-r	fr	fr-ĭ	fri	fri-sk	frisk-y

s-t	st	st-ŏ	sto	sto-p	stop
t-r	tr	tr-ŏ	tro	tro-t	trot
f-l	fl	fl-ŏ	flo	flo-p	flop

*It's good to speak straight
But be sure it originates*

*from the SHOULDER . . .
from HIGHER UP!!*

Julie's

Julie's frisky

Julie's frisky kids

Julie's frisky kids creep.

Julie's frisky kids creep, step, slide

Julie's frisky kids creep, step, slip, slide, trip

Julie's frisky kids creep, step, slip, slide, trip, trot

Julie's frisky kids creep, step, slip, slide, trip, trot,

flip, flop, skid, spin—stop—and then *sleep!*

p-l	pl	pl-ă	pla	pla-n	plan-s
p-l	pl	pl-ā	pla	pla-te	plate-s
b-l	bl	bl-ă	bla	bla-ck	black
c-r	cr	cr-ă	cra	cra-b	crab-s
c-l	cl	cl-ă	cla	cla-m	clam-s
f-l	fl	fl-ā	fla	fla-ky	flaky
g-r	gr	gr-ā	gra	gra-pe	grape-s

F-r	Fr	Fr-ĕ	Fre	Fre-d	Fred
f-r	fr	fr-ĕ	fre	fre-sh	fresh
g-r	gr	gr-ēe	gree	gree-n	green
c-r	cr	cr-ēa	crea	crea-m	cream
t-r	tr	tr-ēa	trea	trea-t	treat-s

p-l	pl	pl-ŭ	plu	plu-m	plum-s
c-r	cr	cr-ŭn	crun	crun-ch	crunch-y
p-r	pr	pr-ū	pru	pru-ne	prune

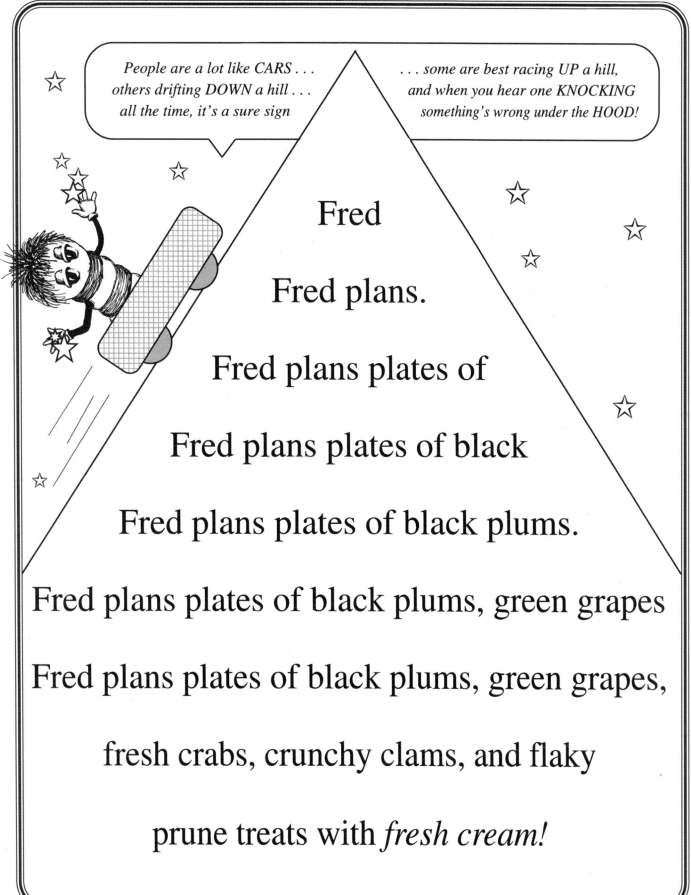

People are a lot like CARS . . .
others drifting DOWN a hill . . .
all the time, it's a sure sign

. . . some are best racing UP a hill,
and when you hear one KNOCKING
something's wrong under the HOOD!

Fred

Fred plans.

Fred plans plates of

Fred plans plates of black

Fred plans plates of black plums.

Fred plans plates of black plums, green grapes

Fred plans plates of black plums, green grapes,

fresh crabs, crunchy clams, and flaky

prune treats with *fresh cream!*

R-Modified Vowels

When vowels are followed by the letter "r" they makes new sounds, which are neither short nor long. This new sound has been modified by the letter "r." The diacritical mark for an r-modified "a" in words like "park" is called an "umlaut," and looks like this: ar=är

The diacritical mark for "or" As in "pork" is called a "circumflex," and looks like this: ôr. There are many spellings for this sound:

or (pork), ar (warn), oor (door), ore (more), our (four), oar (soar)

But the diacritical mark for "or" as in "work" looks like this: ʉr. There are many different spellings for this sound as well:

Whew!

or (work), er (fern), ir (bird), ur (burn), & ear (pearl)

är	M-ar	Mar	Mar-k	Mark
är	h-ar	har	har-d	hard
är	ch-ar	char	char-d	chard
är	g-ar	gar	gar-den	garden
ôr	c-or	cor	cor-n	corn
ôr	n-or	nor	s-nor-es	snores
ôr	p-or	por	por-ch	porch
ôr	w-ar (ôr)	war	war-m	warm
ʉr	n-or (ʉr)	nor	Con-nor	Connor
ʉr	w-or (ʉr)	wor	wor-k	work
ʉr	F-er (ʉr)	Fer	Fer-n	Fern

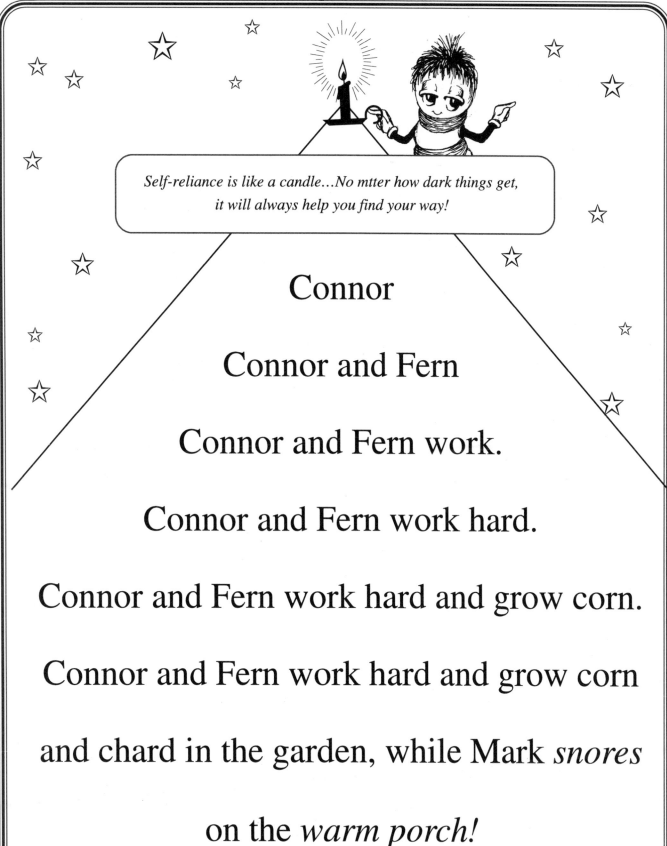

Self-reliance is like a candle...No mtter how dark things get, it will always help you find your way!

Connor

Connor and Fern

Connor and Fern work.

Connor and Fern work hard.

Connor and Fern work hard and grow corn.

Connor and Fern work hard and grow corn

and chard in the garden, while Mark *snores*

on the *warm porch!*

All of the words on this page have the "ur" sound, even though they are spelled in many different ways:

er	G-er	Ger	Ger-t	Gert
er	H-er	Her	Her-b	Herb
er	f-er	fer	fer-n	fern
er	p-er	per	per-fect	perfect

| or | w-or | wor | wor-ms | worms |

| ir | f-ir | fir | fir-m | firm |

| ur | b-ur | bur | burn-t | burnt |
| ur | t-ur | tur | tur-n | turn |

ear	s-ear	sear	sear-ch	search
ear	ear-th	earth		
ear	p-ear	pear	pear-l	pearl

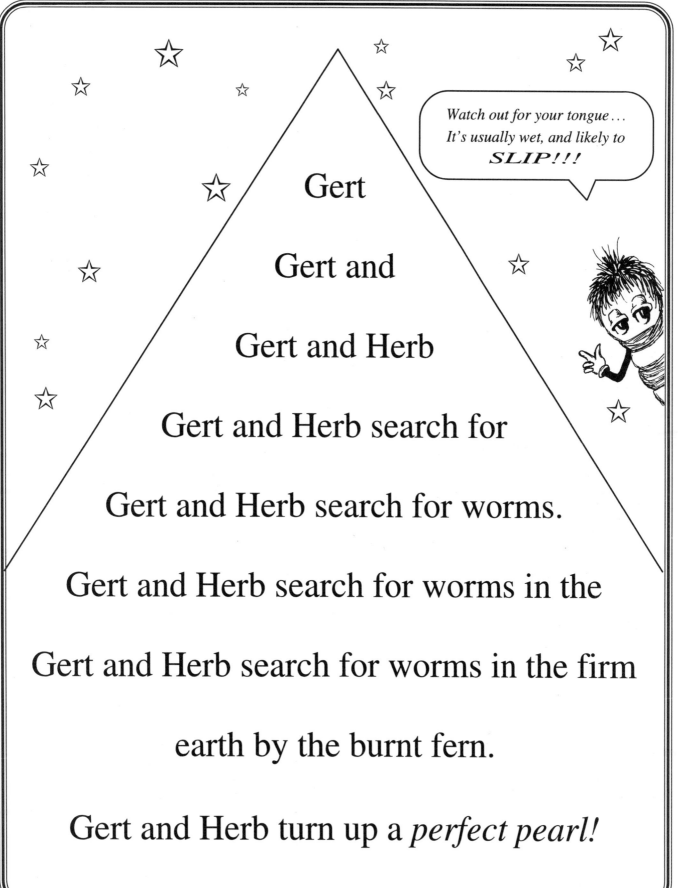

*Watch out for your tongue...
It's usually wet, and likely to*
SLIP!!!

Gert

Gert and

Gert and Herb

Gert and Herb search for

Gert and Herb search for worms.

Gert and Herb search for worms in the

Gert and Herb search for worms in the firm

earth by the burnt fern.

Gert and Herb turn up a *perfect pearl!*

är	sh-ar	shar	shar-k	shark
är	sm-ar	smar	smar-t	smart
är	d-ar	dar	dar-k	dark

ur	l-ur	lur	lur-ks	lurks
ur	m-ur	mur	mur-ky	murky
ur	c-ur	cur	cur-ls	curls
ur	t-ur	tur	tur-ns	turns
ur	b-ur	bur	bur-sts	bursts
ur (ear)	s-ear	sear	sear-ches	searches

ôr	f-or	for	for-th	forth
ôr	st-or	stor	stor-my	stormy
ôr	sn-or	snor	snor-ts	snorts
ôr	p-or	por	por-k	pork
ôr (oar)	s-oar	soar	soar-s	soars

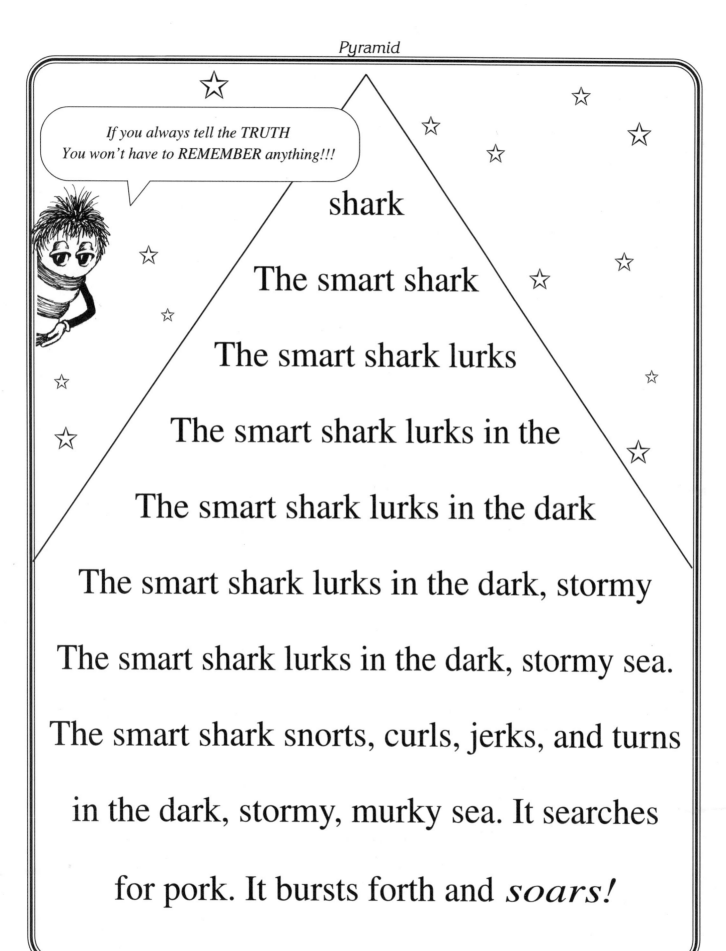

If you always tell the TRUTH
You won't have to REMEMBER anything!!!

shark

The smart shark

The smart shark lurks

The smart shark lurks in the

The smart shark lurks in the dark

The smart shark lurks in the dark, stormy

The smart shark lurks in the dark, stormy sea.

The smart shark snorts, curls, jerks, and turns

in the dark, stormy, murky sea. It searches

for pork. It bursts forth and *soars!*

Long-Vowel Digraphs

Digraphs are two letters that make one sound. This lesson will present practice with long-A and long-E digraphs: (No, "Y" isn't a digraph, but it sounds like long-E!)

ā=ay (play), ai (pail)   ē=ie (field), ies (kitties), y (baby)

ay	pl	pl-ay	play
ay	gr	gr-ay	gray
ay	str	str-ays	strays
ay	cr-ay	cr-ay-fish	crayfish

ai	fai	fai-nt	faints
ai	trai	trai-l	trail
ai	pai	pai-l	pail
ai	frai	frai-l	frail

ie	Ka	Ka-tie	Katie
ie	Deb	Deb-bie	Debbie
ies	kit	kit-ties	kitties
ies	pan	pan-sies	pansies
y	car	car-ry	carry

The DISTANCE we travel is not as important as the DIRECTION!!!

Katie

Katie and Debbie

Katie and Debbie carry

Katie and Debbie carry a pail.

Katie and Debbie carry a pail of frail

Katie and Debbie carry a pail of frail gray

Katie and Debbie carry a pail of frail gray kitties

on a trail in a field of pansies and play.

A kitty strays away on the trail and gets bit by

a big, mean crayfish. Katie *faints!*

Here are the rest of the long-vowel digraphs. Most but not all of them are used in the practice sentences that follow:

$\bar{o}$=oe (Joe), oa (road), ow (slow) $\bar{i}$=y (spy), uy (buy), ui (guide)

$\bar{u}$=oo (moon), ue (Sue), ui (cruise), ou (you), o (do), ew (few)

sl	sl-y	sly		
sp	sp-y	spy		

oe	J-oe	Joe		

oa	c-oa	coa	coa-st	coast
oa	r-oa	roa	roa-d	road

ow	sl-ow	slow	slow-ly	slowly
fo	fo-l	fol	fol-low	follow
sh	sh-a	sha	sha-dow	shadow

oo	m-oo	moo	moo-n	moon
oo	st-oo	stoo	stoop-ing	stooping

ue	S-ue	Sue		
ue	bl-ue	blue		

ui	cr-ui	crui	crui-se	cruise

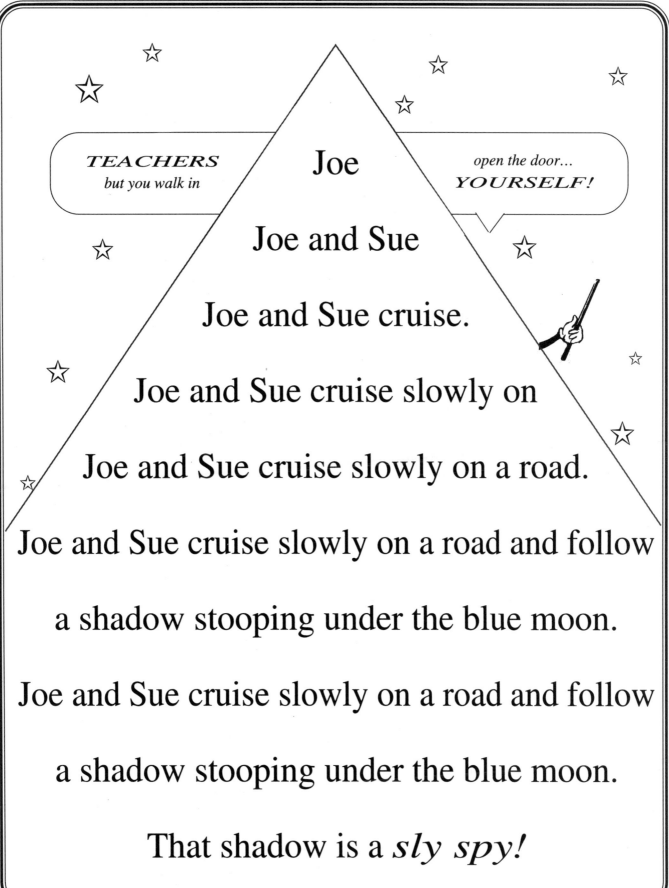

TEACHERS
but you walk in

Joe

open the door...
YOURSELF!

Joe and Sue

Joe and Sue cruise.

Joe and Sue cruise slowly on

Joe and Sue cruise slowly on a road.

Joe and Sue cruise slowly on a road and follow

a shadow stooping under the blue moon.

Joe and Sue cruise slowly on a road and follow

a shadow stooping under the blue moon.

That shadow is a *sly spy!*

Multisyllable Word Pyramids

In this section of *Pyramid* we shall practice building small words into longer ones, by adding syllables. (Syllables are the parts into which longer words can be divided. Each syllable contains one vowel sound—that's how you can always tell how many syllables there are in a word.) The small word on top builds by syllables into the long word on the bottom of each *Pyramid*. The longest word in the world can be read *easily,* once it is broken up into syllables!

There is one word in each *Pyramid*, and two *Pyramid* words are incorporated in each sentence. Read the first *Pyramid*, and then write it from dictation. Repeat with the second *Pyramid* for that sentence, and then read the sentence itself. It's fun to "build" long words, and it's interesting to read them in sentences! With practice you will be able to read them faster and faster—perhaps on sight. Take your time, though—your focus right now is on learning how to *read* long words, not on trying to read them *fast*. Speed will come later, with practice.

You may not understand what some of these words mean. Look them up in the dictionary! Not only will it give you the exact definition of these words, but the diacritical marks used over the letters will help you know how to pronounce them, as will the accent marks over the syllables in this book.

A summary of all seventy-two multisyllable words is on pages 94-95. The original words are all in outline type like this, inside of the multisyllable words.
It's fun to build **V E R Y   L O N G** words from *VERY SHORT* words!

NOTE: Sometimes the middle syllables of a *Pyramid* are real words thermselves and may be pronounced differently, according to how they are read within the final multisyllable word on the next line.*

*For example, in this book "con´-front" has the accent on the first syllable because that is how we pronounce it when we read "con´-fron-ta´-tion" in the next line. But the correct pronunciation for that word without the suffix is really "con-front´."

lent	art
tal´-ent	ar-tis´
tal´-ent-ed	ar-tis´-tic

Margo is very talented and makes artistic paintings.

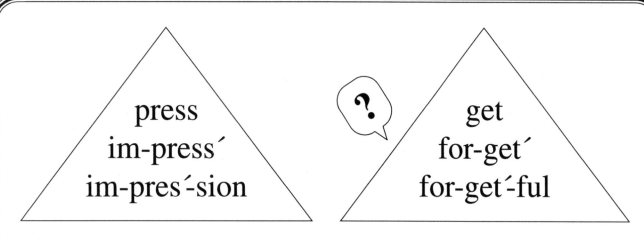

press
im-press´
im-pres´-sion

?

get
for-get´
for-get´-ful

I have the impression that Dor can be a bit forgetful.

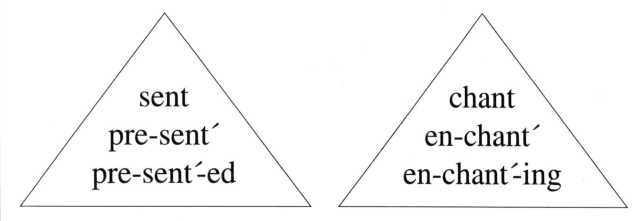

sent
pre-sent´
pre-sent´-ed

chant
en-chant´
en-chant´-ing

Robin presented Chris with an enchanting baby boy.

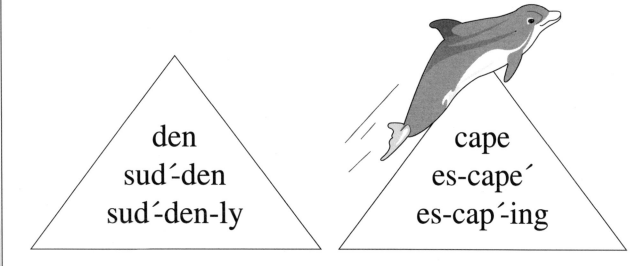

den
sud´-den
sud´-den-ly

cape
es-cape´
es-cap´-ing

Suddenly Andy and Jason see the big fish escaping.

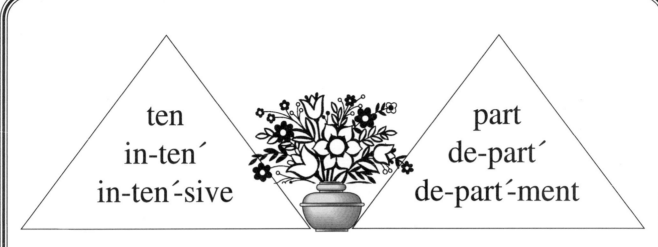

ten
in-ten´
in-ten´-sive

part
de-part´
de-part´-ment

Mom is doing well in the intensive care department.

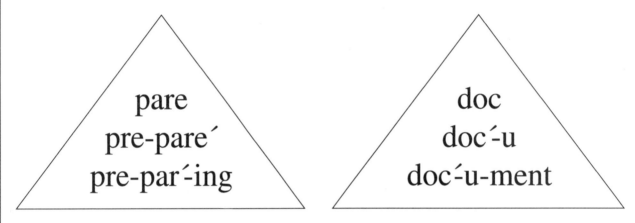

pare
pre-pare´
pre-par´-ing

doc
doc´-u
doc´-u-ment

Barbara is preparing a thick document for Norm.

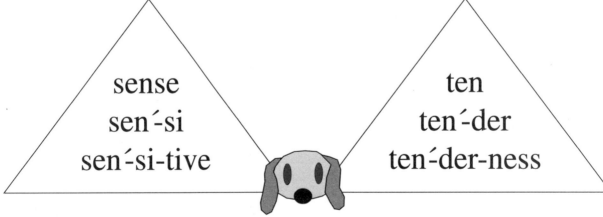

sense
sen´-si
sen´-si-tive

ten
ten´-der
ten´-der-ness

Ruth's sensitive little dog needs a lot of tenderness.

tend
pre-tend´
pre-tend´-ing

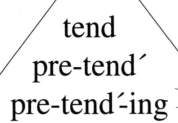

vest
in-vest´
in-vest´-ment

Katie is pretending that the investment is real gold.

tend
ex-tend´
ex-tend´-ing

form
per-form´
per-form´-ance

Derrick is extending Charlie's great performance.

test
pro-test´
pro-test´-ing

gust
dis-gust´
dis-gust´-ing

Brian is protesting the disgusting slug in his mug.

like
un-like´
un-like´-a-ble

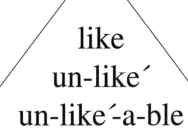

sense
in-sen´-si
in-sen´-si-tive

Steven says snakes are unlikeable, insensitive pets.

hen
pre-hend´
com´-pre-hends´

ice
price
price´-less

Lauren comprehends that the old coin is priceless.

pun
pun´-ish
pun´-ish-ment

fresh
re-fresh´
re-fresh´-ments

As punishment, Gus did not get any refreshments.

land
out-land´
out-land´-ish

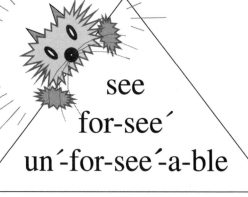

see
for-see´
un´-for-see´-a-ble

Stinson's antics are outlandish and unforseeable.

firm
con-firm´
con-firm´-ing

point
ap-point´
ap-point´-ment

Warren is confirming his ten o'clock appointment.

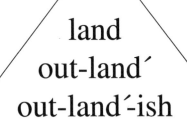

rest
in´-ter-est´
in´-ter-est´-ing

vest
in-vest´
in-vest´-ment

Bob and Patty made a very interesting investment.

won
won´-der
won´-der-ful-ly

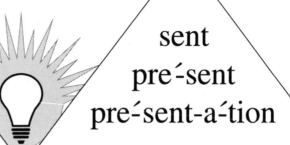

sent
pre´-sent
pre´-sent-a´-tion

Jessie really gave a wonderfully clear presentation.

dent
ci-dent´
ac´-ci-dent´

vent
pre-vent´
pre-vent´-a-ble

She told Marge that the accident was preventable.

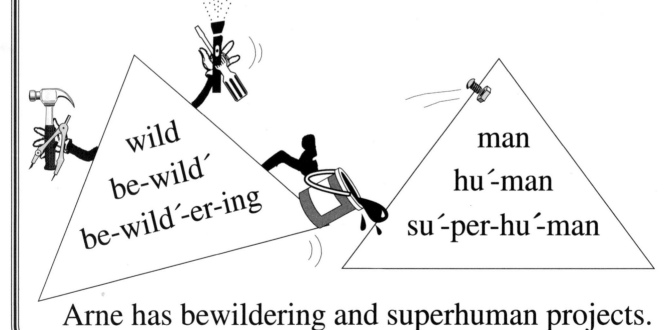

wild
be-wild´
be-wild´-er-ing

man
hu´-man
su´-per-hu´-man

Arne has bewildering and superhuman projects.

rent
cur-rent
con-cur-rent-ly

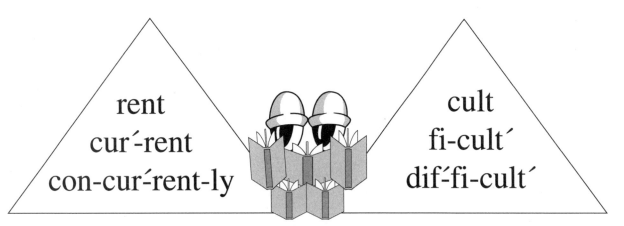

cult
fi-cult
dif-fi-cult

John is concurrently reading five difficult books.

mark
re-mark
re-mark-a-ble

pass
sur-pass
un-sur-pass-a-ble

Linda and Rick do a remarkable, unsurpassable job.

tent
con-tent
con-tent-ed

plate
tem-plate
con-tem-plates

Ally is contented and contemplates her dinner.

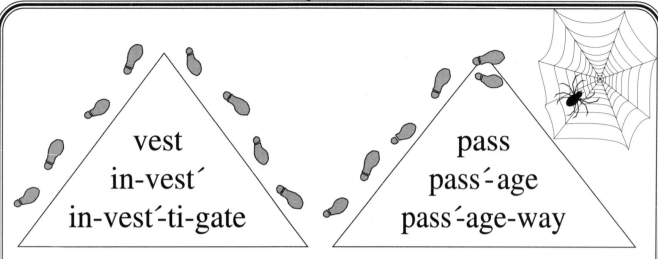

vest
in-vest´
in-vest´-ti-gate

pass
pass´-age
pass´-age-way

Susan will now investigate that deep, dark passageway.

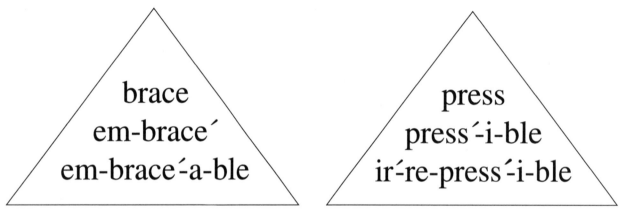

brace
em-brace´
em-brace´-a-ble

press
press´-i-ble
ir´-re-press´-i-ble

Connor is an embraceable and irrepressible toddler.

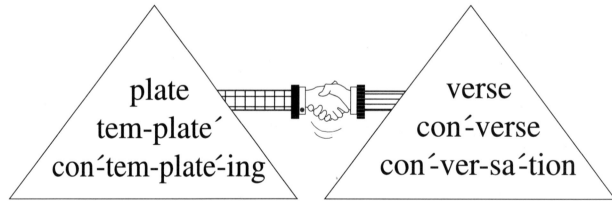

plate
tem-plate´
con´-tem-plate´-ing

verse
con´-verse
con´-ver-sa´-tion

Jay is still contemplating their brief conversation.

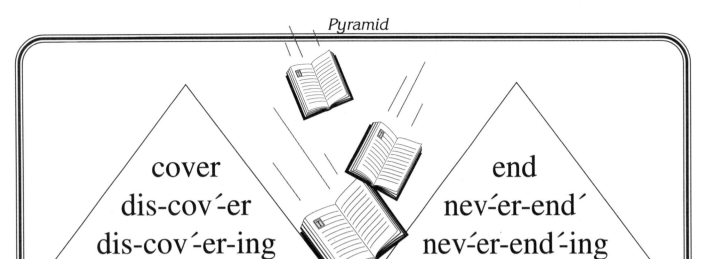

cover
dis-cov´-er
dis-cov´-er-ing

end
nev´-er-end´
nev´-er-end´-ing

Ben is discovering that homework is neverending.

fort
com´-fort
com´-fort-a-bly

part
com-part´
com-part´-ment

Dorothy sits comfortably in the plane's compartment.

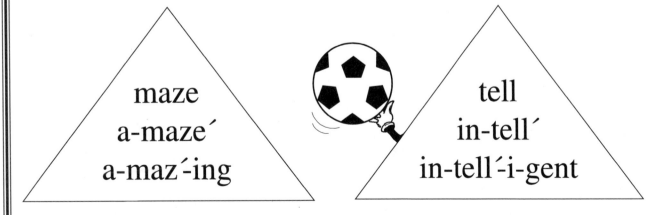

maze
a-maze´
a-maz´-ing

tell
in-tell´
in-tell´-i-gent

Chris is an amazing and intelligent soccer coach.

mark
re-mark´
re-mark´-a-bly

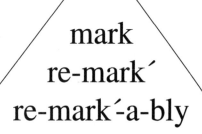

tent
con-tent´
con-tent´-ed

Lily is a plump and remarkably contented puppy.

arc
sub-arc´
sub-arc´-tic

mark
mar´-ket
su´-per-mar´-ket

Julie is freezing in this cold, subarctic supermarket.

cov-er
dis-cov´-er
dis-cov´-er-ing

as
as-tound´
as-tound´-ing

Emily is discovering Dan's astounding drum set.

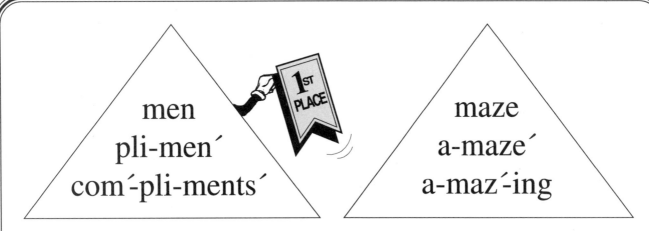

men
pli-men´
com´-pli-ments´

maze
a-maze´
a-maz´-ing

Kim gets compliments for doing such an amazing job.

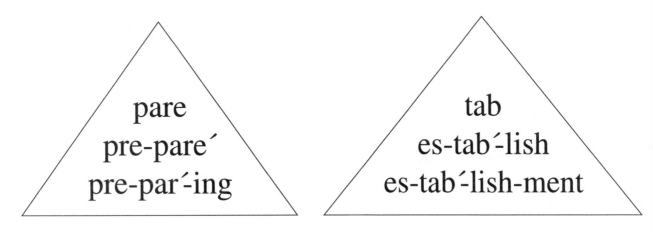

pare
pre-pare´
pre-par´-ing

tab
es-tab´-lish
es-tab´-lish-ment

Courtney is preparing Patti's new establishment.

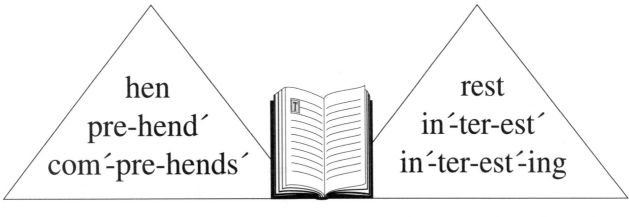

hen
pre-hend´
com´-pre-hends´

rest
in´-ter-est´
in´-ter-est´-ing

Jimmy comprehends Melissa's interesting book.

brace
em-brace´
em-brace´-a-ble

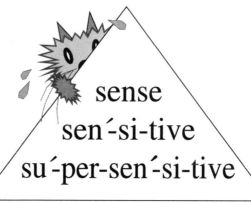

sense
sen´-si-tive
su´-per-sen´-si-tive

Kiwi was an embraceable but supersensitive kitty.

lock
inˆ-ter-lock´
in´-ter-lock´-ing

bin
com´-bin
com´-bin-a´-tion

Jeff and Sharon's lock has an interlocking combination.

rent
cur´-rent
con-cur´-rent-ly

for
for´-mid
for´-mid-a-ble

Lindsay's kids concurrently read formidable books.

fan
fan-tas´
fan-tas´-tic

mem
mem´-ber
re-mem´-ber-ed

Jean was fantastic and will always be remembered.

be
be-gin´
be-gin´-ning

sub
sub-trac´
sub-trac´-tion

Spencer and Re-bec´-ca are beginning subtraction.

pat
com-pat´
com-pat´-i-ble

one
ev´-ery
ev´-ery-one

Mary is much loved and compatible with everyone.

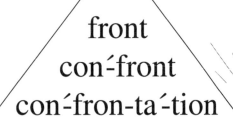

front
con´-front
con´-fron-ta´-tion

cat
del´-i-ca
del´-i-ca-tes´-sen

He had a big confrontation in the delicatessen.

day
yes´-ter
yes´-ter-day

set
up-set´
up-set´-ting

The news on TV yesterday was upsetting to Claire.

flag
con´-flag
con´-flag-ra´-tion

for
un-for´
un-for´-tu-nate

That sudden conflagration was most unfortunate.

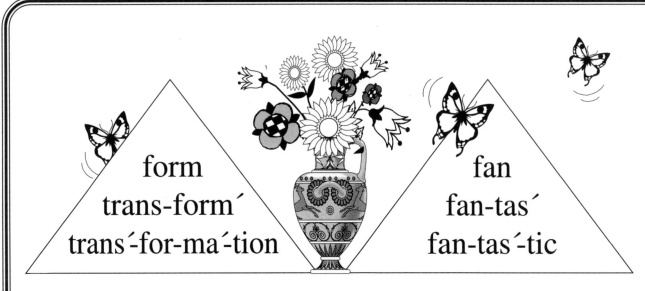

form
trans-form´
trans´-for-ma´-tion

fan
fan-tas´
fan-tas´-tic

The transformation in Robin's home is just fantastic!

math
math´-e-ma
math´-e-ma´-tics

pet
re-pet´
re-pet´-i-tive

Mathematics needs a great deal of repetitive study.

dent
pen´-dent
in´-de-pen´-dent

press
re-press´
ir´-re-pres´-si-ble

Allison and Ryan are independent, irrepressible kids.

path
path-e´-tic
sym´-path-e´-tic

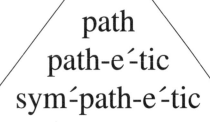

place
re-place´
re-place´-ment

Donna is a truly kind and sympathetic replacement.

duct
in´-tro-duct´
in´-tro-duc´-tion

be
be-wild´
be-wild´-er-ing

His introduction was very odd and bewildering.

sent
sent´-i-men´
sen´-ti-men´-tal

in
in´-ter-con´
in´-ter-con´-tin-en´-tal

John gets sentimental over intercontinental travel.

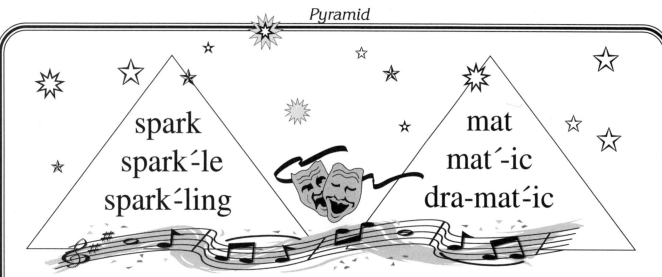

spark
spark´-le
spark´-ling

mat
mat´-ic
dra-mat´-ic

Austen is a very sparkling and dramatic child.

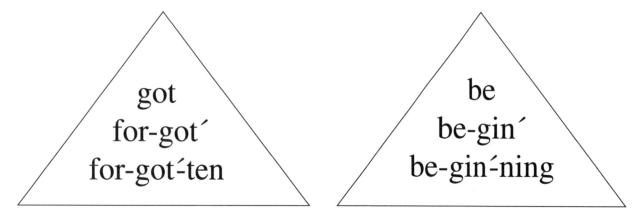

got
for-got´
for-got´-ten

be
be-gin´
be-gin´-ning

Loraine had not forgotten the beginning of the poem.

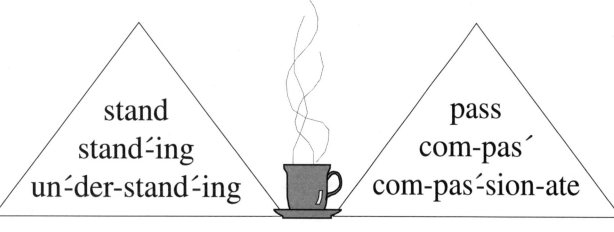

stand
stand´-ing
un´-der-stand´-ing

pass
com-pas´
com-pas´-sion-ate

Olga is an understanding and compassionate friend.

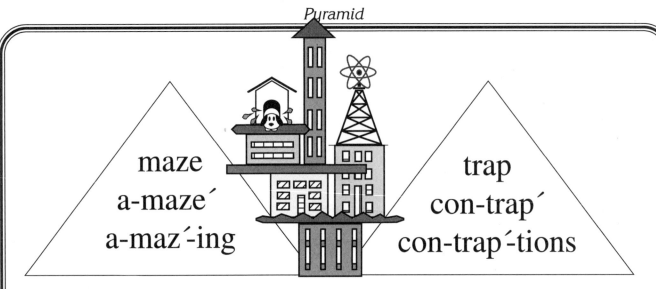

maze
a-maze´
a-maz´-ing

trap
con-trap´
con-trap´-tions

Connor loves to build the most amazing contraptions.

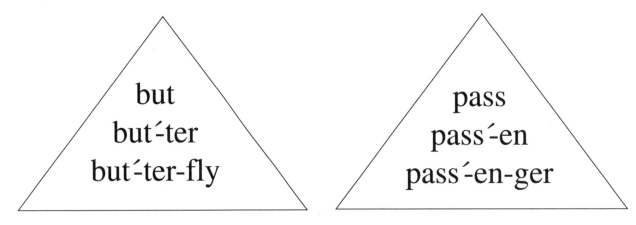

but
but´-ter
but´-ter-fly

pass
pass´-en
pass´-en-ger

Bobby found a blue butterfly on the passenger seat.

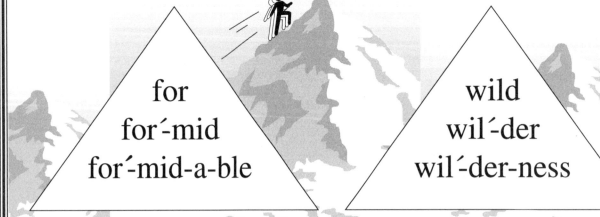

for
for´-mid
for´-mid-a-ble

wild
wil´-der
wil´-der-ness

Jim went on a formidable hike in the wilderness.

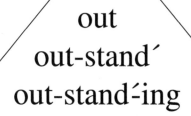

out
out-stand´
out-stand´-ing

pen
dis-pen´
in´-dis-pen´-sa-ble

Dee's outstanding cookies are truly indispensable.

ant
ant´-e
ant´-e-lope

day
hol´-i
hol´-i-day

Cassie saw a tiny baby antelope while on holiday.

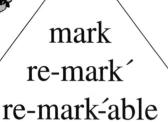

won
won´-der
won´-der-ful

mark
re-mark´
re-mark´-able

Bev was my wonderful and truly remarkable sister.

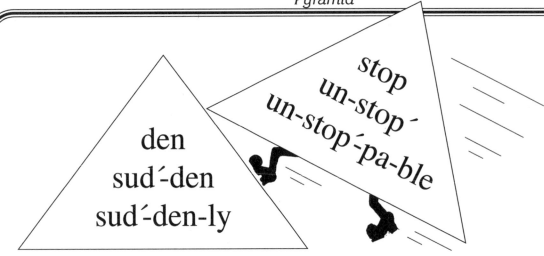

den
sud´-den
sud´-den-ly

stop
un-stop´
un-stop´-pa-ble

Suddenly Lara ran twice as fast and was unstoppable.

red
in-cred´
in-cred´-i-ble

pass
sur-pass´
un´-sur-pass´-a-ble

Pam is an incredible and unsurpassable teacher.

land
out-land´
out-land´-ish-ly

pen
pen´-sive
ex-pen´-sive

Mark's shiny new red car is outlandishly expensive!

pan
ex-pand´
ex-pand´-ing

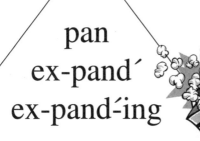

fresh
re-fresh´
re-fresh´-ments

Gus is expanding from eating too many refreshments.

found
foun-da´
foun-da´-tion

force
in-force´
re´-in-force´-ment

Bob and Joy's Foundation has a lot of reinforcement.

press
ex-press´
ex-pres´-sion

chant
en-chant´
en-chant´-ing

Baby Austen's expression is sweet and enchanting.

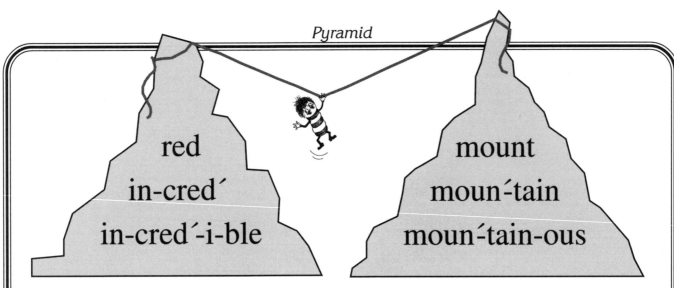

red
in-cred´
in-cred´-i-ble

mount
moun´-tain
moun´-tain-ous

Grant likes climbing incredible, mountainous peaks.

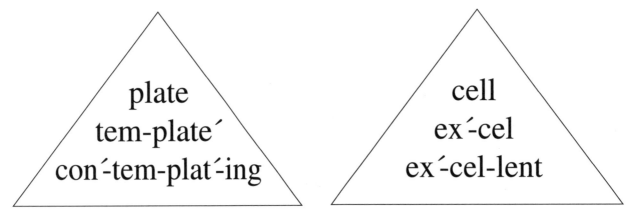

plate
tem-plate´
con´-tem-plat´-ing

cell
ex´-cel
ex´-cel-lent

Jack is now contemplating three excellent choices.

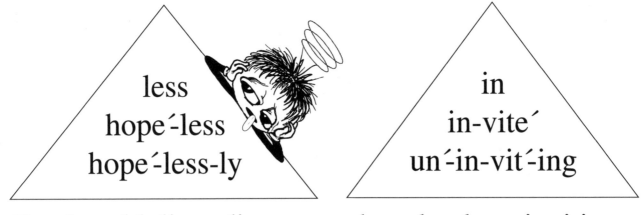

less
hope´-less
hope´-less-ly

in
in-vite´
un´-in-vit´-ing

Don's cold, limp dinner was hopelessly uninviting.

out
out-stand´
out-stand´-ing

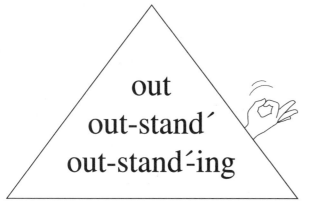

duct
in´-tro-duct´
in´-tro-duc´-tion

Caroline gave a truly outstanding introduction.

press
ex-press´
ex-pres´-sion

late
trans-late´
un´-trans-late´-a-ble

The expression on Jamie's face was untranslatable.

rat
crat´-ic
Dem´-o-crat´-ic

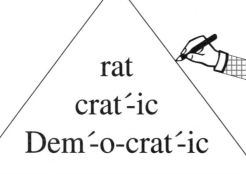

pub
pub´-li
Re-pub´-li-can

Do you think Tot will vote Democratic or Republican?

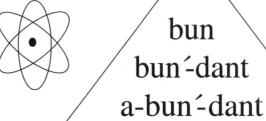

tell
in-tell´
in-tell´-i-gent

bun
bun´-dant
a-bun´-dant

Leslie is very intelligent, and has abundant energy.

prove
im-prove´
im-prov´-ing

round
sur-round´
sur-round´-ings

Molly is greatly improving these surroundings.

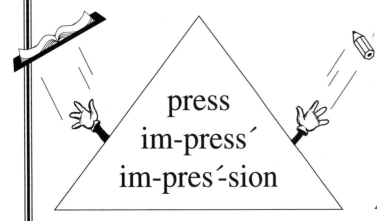

press
im-press´
im-pres´-sion

end
nev´-er-end´
nev´-er-end´-ing

My impression is that, at last, this neverending book is finally finished. This is **THE END!**

. . . *And so ends Pyramid.*

The next two pages contain a summary of all seventy-two multisyllable words used in the exercises we have just finished. Notice that the original, small word is highlighted inside of each longer word. It's so much easier to read long words when you are able to break them down into syllables!

It might be fun to try making up your own sentences using these words. What do **you** *think?*

In any case, just keep on reading—the more that you read, the better you will be able to. You'll see. Your reading will just get

BETTER

and

BETTER

and

BETTER!

Multisyllable Word List

abundant	accident	amazing
antelope	appointment	artistic
astounding	beginning	bewildering
butterfly	comfortably	compartment
compassionate	combination	compatible
compliments	comprehends	concurrently
confirming	conflagration	confrontation
contented	contemplating	contraptions
conversation	delicatessen	Democratic
department	difficult	discovering
document	disgusting	dramatic
embraceable	enchanting	escaping
establishment	everyone	expanding
excellent	expensive	expression
extending	fantastic	forgetful
forgotten	formidable	foundation
holiday	hopelessly	impression
improving	incredible	independent
indispensable	insensitive	intelligent

intensive	intercontinental	interesting
interlocking	introduction	investigate
investment	irrepressible	mathematics
mountainous	neverending	outlandish
outstanding	passageway	passenger
performance	preparing	presented
presentation	pretending	preventable
priceless	protesting	punishment
refreshments	reinforcement	remarkably
remembered	repetitive	replacement
Republican	sensitive	subarctic
subtraction	sentimental	sparkling
suddenly	superhuman	supermarket
supersensitive	surroundings	sympathetic
talented	tenderness	transformation
understanding	unforseeable	unfortunate
uninviting	unlikable	unstoppable
unsurpassable	untranslatable	upsetting
wilderness	wonderfully	yesterday

"There is no vessel like a book

To take us lands away...

Nor any horses like a page

of prancing poetry...

This travel may

the poorest take

without one cent

of toll...

How wondrous is

this chariot

that bears the

human

soul!"

—Adapted from
Emily Dickenson